IGUANODON

A Buddy Book
by
Michael P. Goecke

ABDO
Publishing Company

VISIT US AT
www.abdopub.com

Published by ABDO Publishing Company, 4940 Viking Drive, Edina, Minnesota 55435. Copyright © 2002 by Abdo Consulting Group, Inc. International copyrights reserved in all countries. No part of this book may be reproduced in any form without written permission from the publisher.

Printed in the United States.

Edited by: Christy DeVillier
Contributing editor: Matt Ray
Graphic Design: Denise Esner, Maria Hosley
Cover Art: Deborah Coldiron, title page
Interior Photos/Illustrations: page 5: Luis Rey; pages 8 & 9: M. Shiraishi ©1999 All Rights Reserved; pages 11 & 25: Deborah Coldiron; page 15: Kelly Taylor; pages 16 & 17: ©Douglas Henderson from *Living With Dinosaurs* by Patricia Lauber, published by Bradbury Press; page 19: courtesy of David Goldman, www.copyrightexpired.com; page 23: John Sibbick.

Library of Congress Cataloging-in-Publication Data

Goecke, Michael P., 1968-
   Iguanodon/Michael P. Goecke.
      p. cm. – (Dinosaurs set II)
   Includes index.
   Summary: Describes the physical characteristics and behavior of the spiked-thumbed Iguanodon.
   ISBN 1-57765-634-2
  1. Iguanodon—Juvenile literature. [1. Iguanodon. 2. Dinosaurs.] I. Title.

QE862.O65 G62 2002
567.914—dc21

2001027933

TABLE OF CONTENTS

What Were They?..4

How Did They Move?..8

Why Was It Special?..10

Where Did It Live?...12

Who Else Lived There? 14

What Did It Eat? 18

Who Were Their Enemies? 20

The Family Tree...22

Discovery 24

Where Are They Today? 28

Fun Dinosaur Web Sites 30

Important Words 31

Index..32

WHAT WERE THEY?

The Iguanodon is one of the first dinosaurs anyone discovered. Iguanodon means "iguana tooth." Its teeth look like an iguana's teeth, only much bigger.

Iguanodon
Ig-WON-uh-DON

The Iguanodon was about 30 feet (9 m) long. It was 16 feet (5 m) tall. That is almost as tall as a giraffe.

The Iguanodon weighed up to 10,000 pounds (4,536 kg). A hippopotamus weighs about that much.

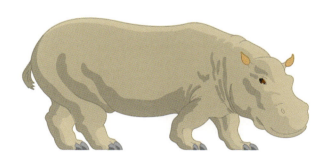

How Did They Move?

The Iguanodon walked on four legs. The Iguanodon ran on its two back legs. It ran faster this way.

TAIL

BACK LEGS

FOOT

The Iguanodon had big back legs. These back legs were thick like tree trunks. The Iguanodon's front legs were small and thin.

WHY WAS IT SPECIAL?

The Iguanodon had a special mouth, or jaw. The Iguanodon could chew food with its special mouth. Some dinosaurs could not chew at all. The Iguanodon could chew better than most dinosaurs.

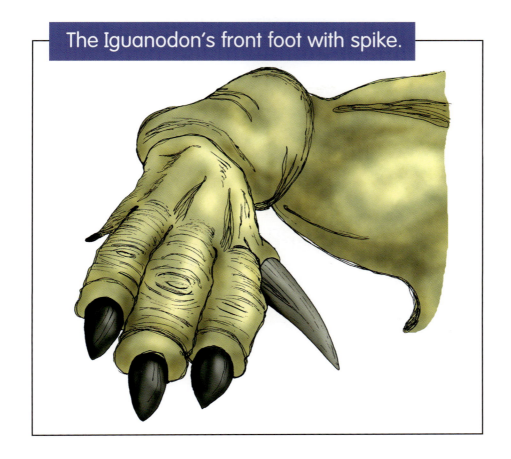

The Iguanodon's front foot with spike.

The Iguanodon had a special claw, or spike, on its front feet. Maybe the Iguanodon used these spikes to grab food. Maybe it used these spikes to fight, too.

WHERE DID IT LIVE?

The Iguanodon lived about 130 million years ago. That was during the early Cretaceous period. Back then, the world was warm and wet. There were a lot of lakes, rivers, and oceans.

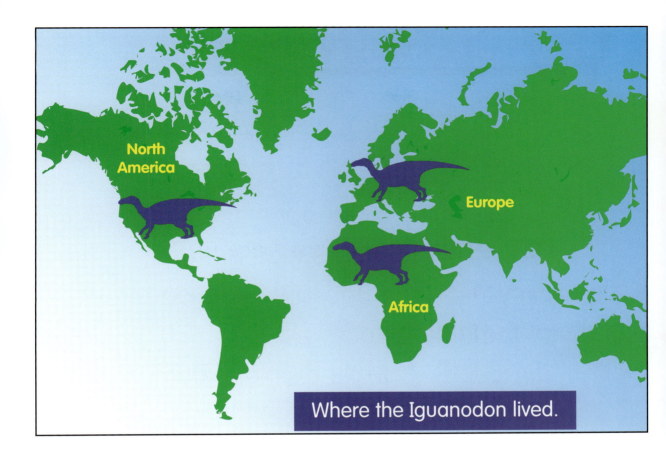

Where the Iguanodon lived.

The Iguanodon lived all over the world. People have found Iguanodon fossils in Europe, Africa, and North America.

WHO ELSE LIVED THERE?

One of the Iguanodon's dinosaur neighbors was the Baryonyx. The Baryonyx was one of the oldest, meat-eating dinosaurs. It walked on its two back legs. Its long mouth was like a crocodile's. The Baryonyx had long claws on its hands. Paleontologists think it used these claws to catch and eat fish.

The Baryonyx

The Iguanodon lived among birds, too. Some of these birds had teeth. The Ichthyornis and the Hesperornis are two of these "toothed birds."

The Ichthyornis lived in groups, or flocks. These flocks nested near water. The Ichthyornis hunted for fish.

A flock of Ichthyornis with a giant crocodile.

The Hesperornis was a swimming bird. It did not fly. The Hesperornis dove underwater and caught squid.

Hesperornis

WHAT DID IT EAT?

The Iguanodon was a plant-eater. It ate cycads and other plants. Cycads are palm-like plants. They do not grow very high.

The Iguanodon grabbed leaves with its beak. This beak did not have teeth. The Iguanodon chewed with teeth far back in its mouth.

The Iguanodon ate plants.

WHO WERE THEIR ENEMIES?

The Utahraptor may have hunted the Iguanodon. The Utahraptor lived in North America. This meat-eater was smaller than the Iguanodon. Yet, the Utahraptor was a good hunter. It had giant killing claws on its feet.

The Utahraptor was smaller than the Iguanodon.

THE FAMILY TREE

The Iguanodon was an ornithopod dinosaur. Ornithopod dinosaurs ate plants. Another ornithopod was the Ouranosaurus.

The Ouranosaurus had something the Iguanodon did not. The Ouranosaurus had a sail. This sail ran down its back and tail. Thin bones held this sail in place.

The Ouranosaurus had a sail on its back.

Discovery

In 1825, Gideon Mantell found some old teeth, or fossils. Gideon thought these old teeth looked like an iguana's teeth. But these old teeth were too big to be iguana teeth. So, which animal did these old teeth belong to?

Gideon thought the old teeth belonged to a reptile. Iguanas are reptiles. Did the old teeth belong to a giant iguana that lived long ago? Gideon thought so.

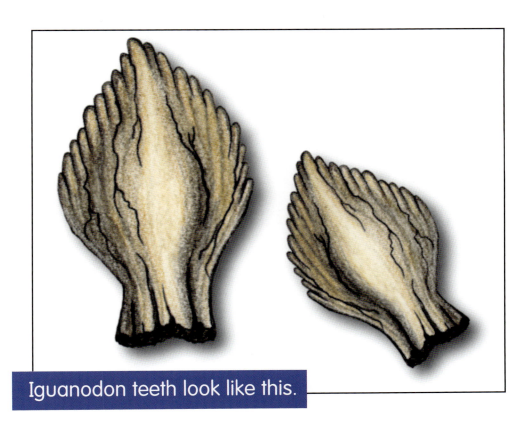

Iguanodon teeth look like this.

These old teeth did not belong to a giant iguana. However, Gideon was right about one thing. The old teeth belonged to an old reptile. But it was a dinosaur. Indeed, Gideon had found the first Iguanodon fossils!

Iguanas are reptiles.

Where Are They Today?

Hunterian Museum and Art Gallery of Natural History
University of Glasglow
Glasglow, G128QQ, Scotland
www.hunterian.gla.ac.uk/

Paleontological Museum
University of Oslo, Norway
Sars gate 1, N-0562
Oslo, Norway
www.toyen.uio.no/

Dick Institute
Elmbank Avenue
Kilmarnock East Ayrshire KA1 3BU
www.mumuland.freeserve.co.uk/

Natural History Museum Nottingham
Wollaton Hall Wollaton, Nottingham
Nottinghamshire NG8 2AE
www.innotts.co.uk/~asperges/woll.html

IGUANODON

NAME MEANS	Iguana tooth
DIET	Plants
WEIGHT	10,000 pounds (4,536 kg)
HEIGHT	16 feet (5 m)
TIME	Early Cretaceous Period
ANOTHER ORNITHOPOD	Ouranosaurus
SPECIAL FEATURE	Spike on thumb
FOSSILS FOUND	USA, Belgium, England, Germany, and North Africa

The Iguanodon lived 130 million years ago.

First humans appeared 1.6 million years ago.

Triassic Period	Jurassic Period	Cretaceous Period	Tertiary Period
245 Million years ago	208 Million years ago	144 Million years ago	65 Million years ago

Mesozoic Era · Cenozoic Era

Fun Dinosaur Web Sites

The Museum
http://www.kbinirsnb.be/general/eng/museum/mus_igua.htm
Read about an Iguanodon fossil site.

BBC Online – Walking with Dinosaurs
http://www.bbc.co.uk/dinosaurs/fact_files/sky/iguanodon.shtml
From the Discovery Channel series, "Walking with Dinosaurs," learn how the Iguanodon walked and what it looked like.

Enchanted Learning.com
http://www.enchantedlearning.com/subjects/dinosaurs/dinos/Iguanodon.shtml
Learn about the Iguanodon's size in comparison to other animals of today and more.

 IMPORTANT WORDS

Cretaceous period a period of time that happened 144-65 million years ago.

dinosaur reptiles that lived on land 248-65 million years ago.

fossil remains of very old animals and plants.

iguana a large lizard that lives in warm, wet places.

paleontologist someone who studies plants and animals from the past.

reptile an animal that breathes air, has scales, and lays eggs.

squid an ocean animal with 10 legs and fins.

Index

Africa, **13, 29**

Baryonyx, **14, 15**

beak, **18**

Belgium, **29**

Cretaceous period, **12, 29**

cycad, **18**

England, **29**

Europe, **13**

fossil, **13, 24, 26, 29**

Germany, **29**

Hesperornis, **16, 17**

Ichthyornis, **16**

iguana, **4, 24-27, 29**

Mantell, Gideon, **24-26**

North America, **13, 20**

ornithopod, **22, 29**

Ouranosaurus, **22, 23, 29**

reptile, **25-27**

sail, **22, 23**

spike, **9, 11, 29**

squid, **17**

Utahraptor, **20, 21**